On the Poetry of Brooke Horvath

"I like Horvath's direct and non-flinching presentations, such as he gave us in his book on Nelson Algren. The poems in *The Lecture on Dust* carry on this personal tradition. The aleatory happenstances of life find their cunning links in Horvath's poetic mind, as in a visit to an eatery, a guy staring at his food, his 'eyes/filling up with bones.' This book has other fine poems, such as the excellent autobiographical rumination on the theory and ethics of fall-out shelters, 'In a Neighborhood of Dying Light,' set around the time of the Cuban Missile Crisis.

"There is evidence of the heartbreak hotel of poesy in these works, but also the determination of plots hidden within plots, which only a poet can explicate in the singular lines of permanence. This is a poet who is able to ask, even in the exploration of the grim nuances of a suicide, 'Why are the plum blossoms always falling?'

"*The Lecture on Dust* is in good part an exploration of the triumph of love and companionship, but it's much more than 'All you need is....' 'What the hell's the deal with serenity anyway?' the poet exclaims in his extended work, 'Shoshaku Jushaku.' Indeed, what's the deal?

"The deal is that poetry is the ultimate exploration."

—Ed Sanders, author of *The Family* and *Tales of Beatnik Glory*

Bottom Dog Press

The Lecture on Dust

Poems

Brooke Horvath

Harmony Series

Bottom Dog Press

Huron, Ohio

Cover painting: *Storm System (Autumn Hwy 115),* oil on canvas, 30 x 60 inches. © 2005, James Lahey < www.jameslahey.com. >
Courtesy of Nicholas Metivier Gallery, Toronto, Canada.
Cover Design: Susanna Sharp-Schwacke
Author photo on cover by Ginny Carroll

Acknowledgments

Apocalypse: Defused or Deferred? (chapbook anthology published by the Poets' League of Greater Cleveland): "In a Neighborhood of Dying Light" (as "Dancing Atop the Berlin Wall"); *Aethlon: The Journal of Sport Literature:* "For a Jogger Attacked in Central Park" and "Men Playing Catch at the Beach"; *Boulevard:* "Open Heart"; *Calapooya:* "July 5th"; *Colorado Review:* "The Lecture on Dust"; *Common Ground: Rebuilding Brick by Brick* (collection published by Kent State University Stark campus Creative Writing Group to raise money for Katrina hurricane victims): "A Cardinal" and "Girl on a Horse"; *Cornfield Review:* "In Ohio" ; *Denver Quarterly:* "The End of Modernism" and "My Grandparents' House"; *Doggerel:* "Physical"; *Elysian Fields:* "Calling Time"; *Great Lakes Review:* "Homeless Man in Mom's Open Kitchen" and "Young Woman Caught Reading in an Easy Chair"; *Interim:* "Paying the Rent" and "A Place Where Nobody Can Follow"; *Jawbone:* "Vacationing Without You"; *Key Satch(el):* "Interview with a Suicide"; *Michigan Quarterly Review:* "Reading *The Gingerbread Man* with My Daughter"; *Our Voices Heard* (chapbook published by PLAN [Planned Lifetime Assistance Network] of Northeast Ohio and Cleveland State University): "A Penny for Her Thoughts"; *The Plough:* "Stopped by the Stars"; *Poetry:* "Winding My Watch"; *Sentence:* "The Green One" and part one of "Shoshaku Jushaku" (as "One Continuous Mistake"); *Sewanee Review:* "Robbing the Dead"; *Spitball:* "Detroit Drops Two to Cleveland"; *Tar River Poetry:* "Leaving the Neighborhood," "Plastic Fantastic Lovers," "Riddle," "Shining My Shoes," and "Stir-Frying"; *Texas Review:* part nine of "Shoshaku Jushaku" (as "Purity"); *Tikkun:* "Ararat from the Flood."
"Reading *The Gingerbread Man* with My Daughter" was also included in *Points of Contact: Disability, Art, and Culture,* ed. Susan Crutchfield and Marcy Epstein (University of Michigan Press).

"Berry Picking," "Death and Old Age," "Detroit Drops Two to Cleveland,"
"Forcing Bed," "In a Neighborhood of Dying Light," "In Ohio," "Snapshot
with Flowers," and "Stopped by the Stars" are taken from *In a Neighbor-
hood of Dying Light*, included in the chapbook collection *Men and Women/
Women and Men* (Bottom Dog Press).

We thank the Ohio Arts Council for their continuing support.

Ginny e,

*Anata o miru to,
itsumo utsukushii shi ga omoi-ukabimasu*

The heart never stops yesterday.

—William Gass

Contents

THE LECTURE ON DUST

I have come to deliver
the lecture on dust

(whose dusty notes are these?
whose ears are burning?)

when your house is burning
learn to love fire

a fiery phraseology my forte
ashes to ashes, I tell them

no fortress can save you
however crenelated, storied

past and future the same story
we live in a continuous present

—thus I make a present of awful
platitudes, grammatical tenses

their tense faces shining up
like sunlight on offal

lighten up, I tell them, face facts
or head for the doors

each is locked, to head or heart
doom's done deal, who struck it?

open your eyes: all thought
however striking, comes undone

neither first thought nor last is best
transparent eyeball, lifted stone

the stone in each chest lifts
splits, repeats: be mine be mine

the mined kingdom is now
and this is, this is, this is it

I

READING THE TAO

I wrote a poem
filled with lies
about your hands,
your voice, your eyes.

I wrote a poem
that was true.
It didn't even
mention you.

SNAPSHOT WITH FLOWERS

A mother holds her child up
against a floral background,
a Botticelli madonna, a Capra still,
a young woman simply proud
or proudly shy.
          The camera saw it all,
stole (to reimburse) a little
of their souls, these long-folded
flowers, the mother's smile,
the child's grin.

          They face us bravely,
these two avatars of hubris,
as though they lived before the fall,
and neither to grow old or die.

OPEN HEART

They are readying to repair
my daughter's leaky heart
that murmurs to itself
like a woeful manitou
watching the horizon
fill with ships.

They are coming ashore
upon the white expanse
of her stunned body, opening
her up, marveling, laying claim,
breaking what will not bend,
mending what they must.

They arrogate her brave
interior, cava and valves,
vessels, veins and cochineal falls.
They will bring back stories
we cannot believe:
Maskanako, Quetzalcoatl.

They are mapping her lush
interior, muttering like the wind
while she lurks elsewhere,
aboriginal and dazed and undivined,
not knowing if the man
whose hands are upon her

is the navigator Brendan,
who will find heaven
in her sacerdotal bones,
Brasail or the Paradise of Birds
in every soporific island
his bruised eyes touch . . .

or godlike Hernan Cortez,
working hard to staunch
the voices stinking in his ears,

hoping for the twin miracles
of wealth and fame,
and up to his elbows in blood.

READING *THE GINGERBREAD MAN* WITH MY DAUGHTER

for Susan

Read, read, as fast as you can
is what I want to say but don't,
for that is what she is already doing
though moving painfully slowly
from word to word as through
something viscous as first
the old woman, then the children,
the horse, the cow, the cat
try to catch the Gingerbread Man.

She is at times a better guesser
than reader, trying
after a peak at the picture
to slip "stove" past me
where the word is "oven."
When I point to ask if that's
the word for "stove,"
she snuggles closer, grins,
says, "Daddy, I believe so."

Sitting on the porch,
we puzzle over morphemes
like two Talmudic scholars,
our reading as labored
as any fundamentalist's,
so tedious I wonder how
she can be following the plot,
its cookie-against-the-world
conflict, its paranoid's vision
of enemies everywhere,
its message of inevitable defeat,
of the brief ripple loss
leaves in its wake,
of indifference to how
the different suffer.
But she croons each "Stop! Stop!"
knowingly, like a seduction,

shouts melodramatically
the hero's brash refusals,
laughs at each escape.
She, too, right now,
would like to get away from me,
but tomorrow must deliver to her class
a report about this horrible story
she has been assigned,
and already, seven weeks
into this new school year,
her teacher, who knows
only one way to teach,
and the principal,
who has said he wants no
"special needs" kids in his school,
have given up on her,
are looking for excuses
to get rid of her.

And so we'll stay here, the book
between us, until the light fails
or we have finished,
although each time anyone
passes on the street,
she must pause to say hello,
to wave and wait for a reply,
which most of the time she gets.
When not, she squints, watching
some jogger or dog-walker pass,
her face screwed up expectantly,
her lips whispering
"hello?   hello?   hello?"
until I recall her to our task,
encourage her to read more quickly,
enunciate more clearly,
as though by speeding through this book
she might outrun her fate,
as though a good report
will change the principal's doughy
smile into something real,

as though knowing which letters
spell "oven" will make true
her teacher's smiling lies
about the school doing all it can.

And so I urge her on
past another foe, the dog
this time, until a clique
of school friends bicycles by
and she must rush to the curb
to call hello. I try
to coax her back, shout
that we've just a few pages left,
but she knows how this story ends,
knows all about the fox
on the last page
who will eat the Gingerbread Man
because after all that is exactly
what gingerbread men are made for.

I yell, "Stop! Stop!"
imitating her, imitating
the old woman, the children,
the horse, the cat, the cow,
her teacher, her principal,
wanting to chase and catch her
so we both can run as fast as we can
and cry to everyone we pass
that they can't catch us.

But I sit, watching the girls
pass by. Each smiles and waves,
but no one stops,
and my daughter stands
a moment longer, arm up,
eyes following, hand moving
in a gesture of greeting
and farewell.

MY GRANDPARENTS' HOUSE

The operative words are dingy, unclean, depressing, grey. Cat hair covers everything. The tv trays are crusted with spilt food, the mahogany dining-room table deep in mail (Clearinghouse sweepstakes years old, newsletters from the Masons, solicitations from the Elks), the chair cushions stuffed with Kleenex, the hassock stacked with newspapers. The cat luxuriates beside the register; it is all they care to talk about: the cat did this, the cat did that. Grandmother lies fetally on the couch in a foul bathrobe, watching *Gilligan's Island,* the volume up, while grandfather, in yellowed under-wear, teeth out, sucks oranges and waits for Merv on the one tv of four that works in the sunroom. The cat strolls sullenly about. Charro stars and is charming. And so we hate to visit, to shout over the televisions, compete with the cat. There is nowhere to sit that is not soiled, dusty, heaped. The air is dry, the hot rooms too close. But that last time I called, I remember how pleased grandmother was to learn we were expecting, and how loudly she laughed out of her small and breathless self when I shouted as a joke, "it's no big deal—what I did, almost anyone could do."

JULY 5th

Last night the sky blossomed with explosions, but they meant nothing and soon died away. Later, bottle rockets, firecrackers. I sat naked in the backyard with a bottle of my own and without fear of observation: I was that invisible. When I looked, even I could not see myself. Ffft. Bang.

Today, the heat continued. I drove into the country to fill a bucket with blueberries and to read the poems of Rabindranath Tagore, a few pages of *The Kural*. Neither was as blue as the berries, or as sweet, but both reminded me that everything worth saying has already been said and that therefore silence is not failure.

Now the berries are in the icebox, the books on the table beside the bed, but at 2 a.m. it is still too hot to sleep. There is silence at the moment and nakedness everywhere. I am on the porch, waiting for the streetlamps to extinguish themselves, for the berries to burst, for something to blossom.

LEAVING THE NEIGHBORHOOD

I am leaving this neighborhood
of shaded streets and well-kept lawns,
obedient dogs, disciplined hedges,
constant home improvement,
and cars washed every weekend.

I am leaving this neighborhood
that decorates itself each holiday,
where ladders are shared, scouts
knock selling magazines and candy bars,
and every little girl's a Brownie.

I am leaving just after the school bus has stopped
and the ChemLawn man has come,
just before the mail arrives
while the widower across the street
bends in his front yard puttering.

I am leaving this neighborhood
where behind each door people talk politely
of high school football or the garden club,
and where, unless in a play,
no one falls out of love with anyone.

I am leaving this street of black squirrels
and birds at feeders, joggers and rollerbladers,
where my neighbor will shovel my walk
if he gets up before I do,
and bikes left out all night are safe.

I am leaving this neighborhood
where I never thought I'd come to live
and now cannot imagine leaving
because behind my door, off-stage, someone
has fallen in and out of love.

DEATH AND OLD AGE

I

On the afternoon we buried grandmother,
grandfather sat in his son's family room,
out of place and almost out of time.
When asked if he'd like to watch tv said,
"How would I know what's on?
I don't get home from work till four"
though he's been thirteen years retired.

At the funeral home had turned
from the shriveled, irremediable coffin
to say how grandmother looked a little better today,
that "she doesn't look old, now does she?"
He calls my father Joe all day,
the name of his brother two years dead,
and calls me Gene, as though
I had already taken my father's place
in the scheme of things.

II

When grandmother died,
we searched her hectic room
for needed papers, found three
strongboxes and, eventually,
their keys.
                Two were filled
with household money,
birth certificates, passbooks,
and the like. The third
held letters and drawings
from my sister and me.
These, too, we learned,
were her important papers.

The contents of box three
(like a bad day

on *Let's Make a Deal,*
her favorite show)
were meager, patient
waiting's doled reward
from two neglectful immortals.

ROBBING THE DEAD

It is a dirty business. Looters disguised
as relatives haul boxes out the door,
like soldiers pillaging a secured village,
murderers disposing of the bloody shirt.

Sheet lightning and thunder like the ghosts
of bombs, but no rain cools the stagnant air
through which tools and lamps and ball gloves
make their way into the trunks of cars.

I look for something white to wave—
this calendar from the last good war,
this autographed ball, this sheet music
whose chords are all suspended ninths.

But everything I touch is yellow as the sheets
beneath the pale blue comforter
on this bed whose mattress keeps the shape
of someone now bodiless as a song.

The piano's keys are yellow, too, their hammers
striking the tense wires softly as the rain
that will not come, catching the apparition of a tune,
then dropping it. There is no one here to hear.

You got lost in a bit of lamp light, your white shirt
yellow against the sky-blue comforter, your ears
full of the sound of your own blood, of water falling,
of tools about their business, of ball meeting glove.

Silence draws itself out where I am, a taut
wire snapped by a slamming door, by the thunder
of someone hammering. Now darkness
begins to sing from each plundered room.

If this were a ball game, it would be the final
inning and, shelled in the eighth, we would be
without comfort with two out and no one on,
and all the runs we'd earned would have been stolen.

Your trunk of uniforms and battle souvenirs
is already gone when someone says, Take whatever
you like. But what? A ball of rain? A lamp
of lightning? This vase filled with thunder?

THE GREEN ONE

I live in the subjunctive, a world of if, perhaps, and could have been. I know the name that names my pain, have chained a line straight to it into sorrow's very heart. What is chained to yours? Hint: the last face you see will not be mine.

I confused self-exposure with self-expression, tousled hair with longing, parlor games for come-ons. Boy, girl. I was a guest on a talk show that nobody watched, and once made the evening news. That was me in the background wearing the embarrassing t-shirt.

You are in Paris, Marrakesh, Bali. You are singing pop songs in Serbian, writing poems to painters, drinking wine along the Seine. I am earning wisdom by mail, one mistake at a time. Power tools, holes in the wall, gin straight from the bottle.

Once I painted a wall where paintings were to be hung, large canvases in blues and greens, reds ands grays. They were all about relationship, the painter said. Later I tore down that wall with a hammer and pry bar. It was all about recidivism.

Drunk, I call your lover but can't stop laughing when he objects to my tone. You are far across that lonesome ocean. I am green and you are grown up. What color does that make you?

Yesterday I spent an hour trying to tape your voice messages to me. "Move the blue one next to the green one," the painter said. The blue one; the green one: I love the way artists talk.

PLASTIC FANTASTIC LOVERS

Found after a storm upon the beach amid a pile of driftwood:
a well-dressed Barbie doll and, unlikely as it sounds, beside her a
small plastic statue of Michelangelo's David.

She didn't mind his nakedness
(she, too, was naked beneath her clothes)
or that he was sexually impaired—
for so was she as everyone knows.

She didn't give a fig for art
but loved to hold his man-sized hand—
just any Barbie with her Dave
alone where waves caressed the sand.

She knew that he could not care less
about her trendy clothes, her fame,
her countless glamorous careers,
or that she was a household name.

They lingered with wood enough to burn
if a cozy blaze were their desire.
If left alone they'll never leave
unless the wind and waves conspire.

But even if the wind should blow
and waves should wash them both away,
their plastic hearts will feel no loss
nor beat less fiercely than today.

THE MAN BESIDE ME

does not eat, but stares
at his food like a dog
at table scraps whose
smell is strange, head
cocked, mouth tight.

The waitress passes,
coos his name, whistles
a laugh, but he just
sits there, eyes
filling up with bones.

STIR-FRYING

I am stir-frying vegetables—
whatever's cheap, in season,
whatever promises health.
Whatever I have.
                    I am fixing
enough for one, methodically,
doing it right, making it last.

I am stir-frying vegetables
because steaming was yesterday
and tomorrow. And as they cook they,
as the old folks say, stir memories—
of all the meals you threw together
from whatever we could find
in the refrigerator, at roadside stands.

Night after night, vegetables,
their storybook shapes and colors,
every night a different combination,
different spices, sauces,
each meal a virtuoso
variation on a theme.

Tonight, with salt and pepper
my only choices,
I am stirring vegetables,
wishing at least one came in blue,
at least one tasted like steak
or Scotch or, better, both.

I am stirring vegetables
in the wok you let me have,
the only pan in which I didn't stick
the girls' scrambled breakfast eggs,
the one in which, feeling gifted once,
I made curried shrimp.

You remember—
you said you liked it
surrounded by wedges of lime
on a bed of cilantro,
served with asparagus
and a bottle of white wine.

I am stir-frying vegetables,
but if you are free this evening,
I would be happy to run to the store.

WINDING MY WATCH

I am winding my watch
because it is an old watch
and keeps old time
of which I am fond—
the time of its making,
the time, just before dessert,
you gave it to me
to commemorate the passage
of ten years' time together,
which was about to have its stop.

It is a thin watch,
which you said meant a good watch,
for you would have even our end
a work of thoughtful elegance.

I am winding this watch
that has outlasted, now, three bands
to show both
how permanent are last things
and how brief a time all things last.

A watch and its band,
once one, then two,
foreverness wed
to replaceability.

I am winding this watch
so it can pass
through its twelve stations
day after day
in its blind sweeping of hours,
its ceaseless sameness,
time heavy on its hands.

A ticking symbol of loss,
this watch catches at my wrist
like a small hand
that won't let go.

A PENNY FOR HER THOUGHTS

She could never
stand up to him,
stare him down,
talk back, talk bad.
He drove her crazy,
and that's no joke.
But for years
before and after
the drugs
and electroshock,
before she was dragged,
screaming,
from her home,
and after her demure return,
when upset she retired
to her room
above the living room
where no one lived,
until, eventually,
retiring became
her vocation.

And that is how,
grandfather ensconced
in the sunroom
before the tv
eating day-old,
half-price pastries,
their bedroom became hers,
where she sat smoking,
rolling her own
thin cigarettes,
muttering, crocheting,
reading Ellery Queen,
Rex Stout, until she
discovered numismatics.

After that, whenever
angered she'd roll

a cigarette and unroll
pennies, nickels, dimes
to squint at their dates,
their condition,
noting the S
that meant San Francisco,
the D for Denver.

Whatever else she did
up there
we never knew
and never asked.
But often when we visited,
above us we'd hear
the plink and roll
of dropped coins,
the creak of her chair
as she bent
over their magnified
minutia.

When she died,
and grandfather died
soon after, we sold
their home to two
do-it-yourselfers
who called one day
to say we ought perhaps
to come over, take a look
at something.
                    We went
to find the living
room ceiling partially off,
the floor deep in debris
with here and there
a green penny, a Mercury dime.
No one spoke
until the new owner said,
"There's a crack
in the floor upstairs,"
then reached up his hammer

to pull off another bit
of plaster and lath,
unleashing as he did
a small storm—tattered
slips of stationery,
matchbook covers,
torn quarter rolls,
all addressed to grandfather,
and each frantic with anger,
with cutting rebuttals,
fierce last words.

SHINING MY SHOES

I am shining my shoes
which I never thought
to shine before,
the expensive leather
weathered and dull,
dog-chewed, salt-stained.

I am shining my shoes
that take me now
up unfamiliar stairs,
into new rooms
in which people only think
they know me,
or know they do not.

To structure the days,
to kill time,
I create small rituals
with pots and pans,
calming bedtime books,
saddle soap and brush.

And so I shine my shoes
that those who knew me,
should we meet,
will conclude
that I am doing fine.
My shoes will tell them
nothing's changed
except for the better.
Old shoes, yes,
the same shoes, yes,
but never looking so good.

I am rubbing and buffing,
my fingers slick and stained,
wax like dried blood
thick under my nails,
so that having hit the road,

the wall, the skids,
 I will not appear
to have hit bottom,
so that running or leaping or standing
dully still
in this dead skin
at least a part of me
will shine.

HOMELESS MAN IN MOM'S OPEN KITCHEN

There's nothing wrong with being bad,
he tells me, if you're good at it—
coming from nowhere to sit beside me
like a gift, a mirror, a payment due.

I was busy breathing second-hand smoke
and drinking coffee from a cup
swiped with some woman's lipstick.
I was busy sweet-talking the waitress
into a free refill. Angel, I said,
but she'd heard it all before, here
where everyone could tell
what I was really doing . . .

And so he sat and told me how he lived
under the by-pass bridge,
how the police never hassled him
but stopped from time to time
to see if he was still alive.
He told me how he weathered
last week's blizzard and this week's
record lows in a sleeping bag,
snowmobile suit, and boots someone
had found for him God knew where.

We talked of shelters and waiting lists,
of how high the river was likely to rise.
He bragged he didn't drink or cuss
but confessed he liked Mom's coffee
and, when he could get them, Swisher Sweets.

Mom had some behind glass beneath the register
beside historic bars of chocolate,
dusty packs of Viceroys—
so I bought him some. Why not?
Because a man with open sores
on hands and cheeks
where the cold has cracked him open,
with hair longer and dirtier than mine,

who can, between the sentences we shared
speak softly to himself things
that shake him with laughter—
such a man deserves a smoke
and needn't worry about cancer
or emphysema, either of which,
or whatever lays him out,
may for all I know descend
like some bright, hilarious angel
laden with gifts
over which he'll laugh
through clouds of sweet smoke
and overflowing Maxwell House mouthfuls,
choking on laughter,
coughing bottomless cups of laughter,
until finally of everything
he's had his fill, until
finally he's famished.

PAYING THE RENT

I am paying the rent
because even though
I cannot afford it,
the rent must be paid.

It is a small task
of grade-school arithmetic,
stamps and a pen that works,
two minutes at the desk.

The check I write is kin
to those that paid
for vacations, groceries, doctors,
your every newest hairdo.

The check I write
still bears your name
next to mine, and an address
where I no longer live.

The check is institutional green,
formal as our conversations.
It wants to know the only thing
that matters now: how much for whom?

Paying the rent, I write hurriedly
like someone checking into
a sleazy motel or signing
a false confession.

Each check is one more step
away from you, a letting
and a letting go, another month
in the nowhere of always.

FOR A JOGGER ATTACKED IN CENTRAL PARK

In the park last night where you were raped and beaten,
did the young buds above you continue singing
their old lies of innocence and rebirth?
And did the young buds, less duplicitous, who held you down
sing anything at all
as the air began to smell as it never had before
and the earth asked harsh questions of your skin?
These boys, when caught, will have their reasons,
or maybe not. Possibly will be better off not having reasons.
Perhaps to them this park said something,
but something they could not understand.
Perhaps like you they sought a challenge they could run to meet,
breathing deeply, the adrenaline rush
urging them to go further than they ever thought
they would or could.

Running is meant to get one somewhere, but not here
where you lie immobile yet erratic in a bed, intimate once more
with things not of your choosing.
You never intended to run for your life like that,
to run scared, never
to run away from, let alone toward trouble. Trouble
that lazily awaited its chance to happen.
And why, despite a catalog of horror stories, here? Here
in the heart of Manhattan, of America,
where surrounded by what we have made of ourselves,
and forgetting the lead pipe, the dishonest outlaw,
the genocide, and a history of unconcern,
we keep alive the myth of what we think we were and wanted
and would be—healthy and free, breathing
the clean air, feeling beneath our feet the good earth.

So this is where you came not knowing this
was a night of wilding, here,
where life does not so much advance
as curve perennially back upon itself,
like this path that brought your running to a stop,
that left you in fragments rudely forced.

And those who chose to punctuate you thus could only, one imagines,
speak in expletives and doggerel,
devil-headed hipsters beneath a fourth-month moon,
though for us all they do and mean
must end in question marks.
What got their hearts to beating fast as yours?
And in their sudden spring, what part did April play,
its green flowering beneath the sun's soft touch
on this racing planet that always ends where it began?

Just so, you came into our lives, then went:
yesterday an unknown jogger through the park,
today news at which we feel or feign outrage,
tomorrow a failing memory of passing unpleasantness.
We have heard about such things before and will again.
We must and do forget. So it happens.
But today it is *your* story
fills a column in the morning papers,
and we ask ourselves the usual mundane questions,
provide the usual lame answers,
though on the outbound trains by evening
beneath the moon-bright sky we share
riders homeward bound nod silently and try
instead to understand
how the Yankees lost, and why.

A PLACE WHERE NOBODY CAN FOLLOW

My picture should be on milk cartons
I am that lost, though no one notices.
No one seems aware the mirror is blank
when I stand before it, striking one pose
and then another, like some vain survivor
of Hiroshima, wondering about this hair
that pulls away in clumps like matted leaves,
this curdled skin, these hollows around my eyes
like two holes drilled into the stony sky.

My portrait should be clipped and hung
in every post office and precinct house,
for I am guilty of something, though of what
I cannot say—of poisoning the milk
of human kindness with my medusa stare,
of failing to be there when the cards and flowers
arrive, of littering this neighborhood
with the debris of my disappearance, clues
that blow along the streets like fallen leaves.

No one seems aware my glass of milk
remains untouched, my mail unopened.
Nobody sees the frightful hole at the window
when I think to look out on a world
where all the trees have been forced to strip
and all the healthy birds have packed their bags
and left. I watch the evening wrap a soiled gown
about itself and take to bed, feverish
from an inflammation of zinnias.

My picture should be hung in every Dairy Mart
until the world becomes my mirror
and every leaf cries out my name;
until everyone recognizes this neighborhood
for the rogue's gallery it is, and every heart
confesses its sour crime of health.
But all the houses are empty, and if the streets
are deep in missing persons, none
is a survivor, and all are stone.

PHYSICAL

1. Urine Sample

They treat my tiny cup of piss
like it was performance art.

2. The Table

One is now a country occupied,
another's occupation, another's victim,
the site of ultimate taboos.

One is now a code to be broken,
a sausage stuffed with sausage,
a shirt turned inside out.

One is now the definition of pornography,
a man without means, the voyeur's
wettest dream, the voyeur's nightmare.

3. Blood Pressure

The least of my worries.

4. Otoscope

A bug in the sluttish ear,
an easy penetration,
aural sex.

A lighted probe
down vacant streets,
along empty canals.

Where *are* the sounds of yesteryear?

5. Reflex Test

Proof one's responses are knee-jerk.

6. Tongue Depressor

The story: brief, tasteless.
The style: flat, clinical.
The dialog: garbled.
The setting: cavernous, symbolic.
The dominant trope: onomatopoeia.
The protagonist: wooden.
The theme: anyone can be somebody's fool.
The moral: avoid being French-kissed by a tree.
The point-of-view: second-hand omniscient.
The denouement: ambiguous.

7. Blood Work

No woman I have slept with
has left me quite so light-headed.

8. Stethoscope

A wiretap on the heart,
covert intelligence,
one blind man's bluff,
a dangerous liaison.

Cough, and give yourself away.

9. Thermometer

Sometimes a cigar
is just a cigar.

10. Latex Gloves

For the prevention of disease
and the encouragement of fear,
a stylish but optional part
of the fetishist's ensemble.

(Don't you wish your parts were optional?
Don't you wish you weren't?)

11. Prostate Exam

I should, perhaps, have brought flowers.

12. X-Ray

No one has ever been so explicit
in giving voice to her desires:
she tells me what to take off,
how to pose and for how long,
when to move.
                Not satisfied
with what there is of me to see,
she wants my bones, my cloudy lungs.

13. EKG

Further evidence
that we are the monster,
not the scientist;
not beauty,
but the beast;

further proof
that induction has its limits,
that there is a demon
in the box
and a ghost in the machine.

VACATIONING WITHOUT YOU

I am vacationing without you,
drinking bottled beer
and puzzling out crosswords
in a one-week summer rental,
walking a beach crowded
with families and men fishing,
but lost in a late fall evening
full of traps and victims.

I am trying to read a book
begun eight months ago,
but its stoic, blind protagonist
is barely there
behind the plot of last November,
its sadder story
and gut-wrenching heroine.

I am trying to take a picture
with the camera last used
when we vacationed
last year, but its focus
is stuck on infinity,
its lens fogged
with images of you.

I am wearing the shorts
I wore last summer, sand
in the pockets still from shells
you found and asked me,
please, to carry home for you.
I have them here, safe
and good as new. Look—
I have pressed them
like snapshots
between the pages of this book
with the happy ending.

LOOKING OUT THE WINDOW DURING A COMMITTEE MEETING

Corked longing for Polly, for Ann,
for broader, less dogged definitions

for long, definite mornings, dog days,
ladies' nights, hazy and buoyant

where dazed beside the brook like treed
longing, lazy boys dog summer

watch corks bob, brook no tacky
pollyanna words of mourning

broad-minded, they stay on top
of what is beneath them—Polly, say . . .

nothing more and never mind—
no parroted words, no quorum

just unquarried sun above
tactless ladies, boyless trees

INTERVIEW WITH A SUICIDE

You chose to gas yourself because . . . ?

Because nothin' says lovin' like someone in the oven.

Wasn't there something we could have done?

Don't flatter yourself.

Why did you do it?

Because the plum blossoms were falling. Because it was so cold on the Ring of Fire. Because my team lost and because all the pilot would say was that we'd be on the ground shortly. Because my girl left and now there is no here. Because the moonlight went crazy in the bedroom and the sunlight was so loud.

Did you make your peace with God?

No: why should God be the exception?

What can you tell us from the other side?

The bright light is a "No Vacancy" sign, and among those who come to meet you there is no one you were hoping to see—they all still want something, and they are never out of debt.

How do you want to be remembered?

That, I believe, is called begging the question.

Anything you'd like to ask?

Who was that woman dancing in my shower, naked beside me when the roads got dark? What was that sound that woke me every night, and who was the caller who always hung up? Why were the lights on when nobody was home? Why are the plum blossoms always falling?

II

SHOSHAKU JUSHAKU

*"Shoshaku Jushaku means 'to succeed wrong with
wrong,' or one continuous mistake."*
                        —Shunryu Suzuki

I

One continuous mistake: to be the good son, good brother, good friend, good
father. To go to work, work hard, eat right, exercise, rake the leaves and fix
the leaky pipes. To row the canoe, coach third, give up my seat. To sit zazen
agreeably. Not to attempt to be more than a friend to the woman whose
smile is heart's ease itself, not to cross the line but to say "this far and no
farther." To attend to the wise and tend the small. To hold my tongue, hang
fire, turn the other cheek. To be prudent, reasonable, patient, forgiving. To
be nice, to try.

One continuous mistake made with perfect single-mindedness: but if that
woman ever again says she hates dressing up to go alone to the symphony,
I will tell her that I will dress up and go with her, gladly. Or, if undressing is
required, then there, too, I will say, I am your boy.

One continuous mistake: these hands that have done so many nice, pathetic,
futile things; these hands that long to bring their emptiness to her form, to be
mistaken there continuously.

II

"There is no other way of life than this way of life."

I wait for your knock upon my door, concoct reasons to stand before
yours.

I hang on your words, in a gush of triteness tell myself stories about us.

What might we do that you have never done before? How long might I
hold you before you felt safe, before you never again want to beat on the
windows in despair of life's unbearable sameness?

I listen as you call me your buddy, tell me you cannot make up your mind. Cliches and soap-opera and illicit, unwelcome yearning.

This is my true nature, to be a ghost attempting to unlock delusion with delusion.

I know there is no other life for me.

III

*"We can say either that we make progress little by
little, or that we do not even expect to make progress."*

This morning I awoke to an image of you beneath trees. I was not there. Your lips did not part for me. Your desires did not spell my name.

Thus I come closer to you, little by little.

When I have abandoned all plans, all desire, will I be closer still?   Even now I search for you in the heart's bloody chambers. Thankfully, the blood is only mine. You are safe elsewhere beneath the oaks, the cool sycamores.

I care for you this much.

IV

*"Bowing is a very serious practice. You should be
prepared to bow, even in your last moment. . . ."*

Here in my final moments I find myself still falling. For you. At your feet. For that.

I peeled my heart to lay it at your feet, then slipped upon it, a would-be monk gone Chaplinesque.

Hungry for the space between your lips, for something to light the heart's dim cell, I offered you a few words, dark beer, jokes and self-deprecation. Desire's pratfall.

You did not laugh but offered me a story. The story was a cliff. There was a sign at the top. It read: jump.

I watch myself fall from where I lay sprawled foolishly before you, my heart going green, yellow, brown. From very far away I hear my true nature calling.

Quickly, tell me your story again, that I might learn at last to bow.

V

"If it really does not matter, there is no need for you even to say so."

It doesn't matter: it is all right. By which I mean it is not all right. By which I mean that it is all right.

Where was I since we became friends? Dismantled in love, away. Thinking you thought me awful. Your cynic. No time even for coffee together. You thinking I thought you bothersome. Sometimes my therapist. Then suddenly this. "You ask me something I can't answer right now." It is all right.

I sit here buried in fantasies, daunted, unable to find the off switch. To walk away. Knowing what I ought and mustn't but writing this, if not to sway you, then why? Bathos, banality: wearing sin like a ring of beauty, dreaming with tears in my eyes. Don't think twice, it's alright.

I will draw back into the proprieties of friendship. How are you this morning? How was your trip? Want a Good & Plenty? The right thing to do, but not all right.

Is it cruel for me to write you and want to talk to you? But what hurts more: emptiness or overfullness? Even if dumped and left to rot, aren't the apples what the trees had to do? But again, to stand at your door every day with more poisoned fruit can't be right.

So it is all right. Of course it is all right. By which I mean I think maybe nothing is ever all right. By which I mean I can't imagine it could ever be entirely not right. By which I mean it matters.

VI

We do nothing. Day after day we realize our true natures. Our nothing
covers everything I do. I remain sitting quietly in my room. To leave, to
move, to think would be unhappiness. I expect nothing. I am the stone for
which the trees are just passing through.

I write you letters, this letter. Schopenhauer wrote, "If you want to know
how you really feel about someone take note of the impression an unex-
pected letter from him makes on you when you first see it on the doormat."
Were I doing anything, I would be wondering what impression the arrival of
these words made on you.

I leave work early, leaving you a message that says nothing. Before you go
home, you leave one for me. The next day, although Saturday, I come to
work, wanting to see if there is a message from you. It says almost noth-
ing, says to call if I like. So I leave a message for you, and later I call but
do not reach you. We are doing nothing. We are expressing ourselves.

Last night, I listened to your latest message, over and over. I listened to
you tell me nothing in a voice so soft, so gentle, so small that when you
spoke your name it was not sound but a blown kiss. Or so I thought, so I
wished to believe, but trying to do nothing. To hear you express nothing.

Your eyes, your demeanor, your true nature: I am not able to handle such
complicated texts. I am stuck on your voice like a child learning to read. I
know only the present tense and have forgotten what the word "friend-
ship" means. No child ever wanted to understand so difficult a text. No
child ever had so much trouble expressing himself. No child has ever been
capable of doing nothing.

VII

We have shared private jokes, meals, a relationship rich in innuendo. We glanced away, stepped back. We showed each other what parts of ourselves were just the disguise. Now, on whatever log I squat, you'll recognize me.

You wrote letters, leaving blanks where the terms of endearment belonged. I praised your indirection, you my indiscretion. You kissed my shameful hand. I kissed your hair. You left me alone with your purse once, and I didn't take or touch anything.

I am wondering: what the hell's the deal with serenity anyway?

Tonight only one child is up late, wearing his usual disguise, doing whatever he is doing. He is stacking words like blocks and calling it poetry. He is playing peekaboo with what he pretends doesn't matter. Now he is recalling how, when he left you alone in his heart once, you touched but didn't take a thing.

VIII

*"By purity we do not mean to polish something, trying to make
some impure thing pure. By purity we just mean things as they are."*

Because I do not listen for you, I hear you everywhere. Only if I look for you is this purity broken, only then do you vanish. Because I do not attempt to see you, touch you, I have no fear of losing anything.

True: at night I think of you until I become too excited to sleep. My thoughts many nights are impure. Night after night I polish these thoughts with no desire to purify them.

Desire was here before I felt it. Then I felt it and made its sounds. Now things with me are just as they are.

Perhaps one day I will find you at my door: how can it be otherwise when you are already and always here? You who cast no shadow upon this purity that burns so completely it leaves no trace. You whose absence means you will never leave me.

If you do come, you will not find me anywhere.

IX

*"Knowing that your life is short, to enjoy it day after day,
moment by moment, is the life of 'form is form, emptiness emptiness.'"*

form is form &
life is short &
emptiness surrounds

in the quiet
bar-dark, dark
beer after dark

& you laughing
growing quiet
telling me

about your day
fragments
of your life

shared with plates
of food
another round

when it comes
when you lean
toward me

smile, reach
to touch
my arm

my hand
it is almost
enough

III

CALLING TIME

Rollie Sheldon holds a wristwatch to his ear.
Ralph Houk leans in to "help him listen."
Behind the crowds and springtime pepper,
they hear the sound time used to make in 1961.
It seems to please them, Rollie especially,
who must have thought he had a lot of time in 1961
when he went 11-5 in his new Yankee pinstripes,
fresh from college and D-League ball.
The year Roger Maris sent those 61 dogs hunting.

Time had a satisfying sound that summer.
John Blanchard got more playing time.
The time was right for setting records
that might last for quite some time.
Mickey, Ellie, Tony, Whitey—their timing
was right that summer, when time
seemed in suspension, measured only in innings
that were themselves subject to no clock
that wasn't wound by strong arms and gutsy fielding.

Ford Frick and endless talk of a longer season
worked overtime to spoil Roger's record.
He could see it coming (he had good eyes).
Mick, of course, was always ready for the worst,
waiting on aching legs for injury's alarm,
spending the money he saw no point
in saving for some other time,
while Bobby prayed and Yogi joked,
and hot Rollie's watch ticked and ticked.

One evening, late in the season, running
out of time like running out a pop fly—
futility at war with hope, and nothing to be done about it—
Roger called time
at Tiger stadium, stepped out of the box
to watch a flock of Canadian geese
fly across the face of the sky's cool, luminous dial.

IN A NEIGHBORHOOD OF DYING LIGHT

Later I would smile, remembering
as Phil Ochs sang
about how "the cold war was a-gettin' hot,"
and Dylan's hard rain fell repeatedly
from the scratchy speakers of my father's stereo.
Yes, later I would read the helpful books
that explained the strategies, the risks taken,
and later still would tie a red bandana about my head
and march, chanting the chants, walking the walk.
But at the time all I knew—
I was small then, only nine—
was what Dorothy Fuldheim told me
one day at the end of the evening news.

These were the days of duck and cover
when there was and then was not a missile gap,
when the basements of Camelot
held bottled water, hand-operated generators,
first-aid kits, and the Game of Life
(it was a time of easy ironies, so let this one pass).
Maury Wills had just stolen his 104th base,
breaking Ty Cobb's record,
and "Monster Mash" topped the pop charts
before giving way to "He's a Rebel."
The Manchurian Candidate had just been released,
and in Vietnam U.S. pilots had begun to shoot first
and ask questions later.

These were the last fine October days
of Indian summer and touch football
when my best friend Dave still lived behind me
(or I behind him, as he would have it)
and my grandparents lived right next door
where every morning before the sun had risen
grandfather revved his old Dodge into motion.
Here everyone (save the bellicose Scots
with their bagpipes and vicious collie)
was friends with everybody else
in my sugar maple and blighted elm neighborhood

whose streets were named for New England towns
with revolutionary connections.

Dinner was just over, or just ready,
and I was home fresh from winning the west
or getting ready for an hour
of ghost in the graveyard. Outside
leaves fell commie red and chicken yellow,
but the picture on the television set
was black and white
as we listened to how Jack had blockaded Cuba,
calling Moscow's bluff.
And that was when Dorothy came on to say
that it would be both perfectly legal
and morally justifiable to kill anybody
who tried to get into one's fallout shelter.

So as I took off (or put on) my baseball jacket
I thought about killing Dave—
how I'd do it, and if I could—
or shooting my grandparents with my new .410
that had blasted countless rabbits in my dreams
if none in life. And I thought
about the Speichers across the street,
childless, yet arranging every Easter
hunts for colored eggs and, come Christmas,
decking their house and yard with gaudy strings of lights
to please us kids. Would they come banging
on our shelter door, trying to buy their way in
with offers of rides in their new T-bird?

Then, fool that I was, I realized
we had no fallout shelter, and our basement
would be no place to hide: it leaked
an inch of water every time it rained
and would never keep out radiation.
So someone else would be doing the killing.
Dave had everything I wanted then—
motorcycle boots, model clipper ships he pieced together
with tweezers and tedious patience,
a go-cart in his garage, and a pool table

in his rec room. Surely, I thought,
he has a fallout shelter somewhere too,
perhaps the pantry beneath his cellar stairs.

Days passed, and the goblins in the classroom windows
gave way to five-fingered turkeys
while I waited for the bombs to fall,
heard them explode as grandfather's car
rumbled awake, and watched
the sky, mistaking passing planes
for ballistic missiles.
In school I drew jet fighters blazing
toward elaborate crashes into gun emplacements,
the pilots bailing out with flaming parachutes,
while awkward soldiers bled Crayola red and died
as mushroom clouds rose black against
construction-paper landscapes.

Meanwhile, of course, the danger had passed,
but no one told me.
My Cuban Missile Crisis lasted weeks and weeks
while snow fell like festive fallout.
Since then, years have passed,
but it will still take more than happy Germans
dancing atop the Berlin Wall
to tranquilize my cold war shakes.
I still have trouble planning beyond tomorrow,
and every once in awhile on a cold October evening
I feel small again and uninformed,
like the only living boy
in a neighborhood of dying light.

JACK RUBY SHOOTS LEE OSWALD

"Well, it's all over now."
        —Lee Harvey Oswald/The Rolling Stones

Minutes ago he was talking
shirts and sweaters with Capt. Fritz.
Now he seems surprised men
still wear hats like Jack's.
His expression as the bullet hits
would not please his mother—
that round, rude oomph!
as though telling the punch
line to some bawdy joke.

The bullet is what becoming
history feels like; how he
takes it is how he'll be
remembered, is better than
pamphleteering for Castro,
posing with a brace of rifles,
better than Marina whispering
his name. It means the world
to him and it is live and . . .

Someone is calling Jack
a son-of-a-bitch and Oommph!
the children of America,
home from school early,
tv sets awash flickering greys
(no *Flintstones* tonight)
watch as again the gun
and again, and each time Lee
staring at Jack, the camera, us.

As Lee grunts and slumps,
one can almost hear the guitars
tuning up, the choppers, smell
grass, patchouli, jellied gasoline.
There will be fire in the streets
and naked men and women dancing

high as kites, days of rage
and hallucinogenic nights
when all anyone wants is sleep.

All weekend, Jack fires, Lee slumps,
and Jackie clambers from the limo.
The Browns beat the Cowboys 27 – 17,
and the sun sets only to rise again.
It is cloudy; there is rain.
Tossing the *I Ching* tells us only
one more thing we already knew:
when the horses run in the mountains,
the pine needles in the valley tremble.

BERRY PICKING

I

The brief bushes hang heavy with fruit
that stains the plucking fingers red
the baskets fill and bleed

our mouths fill with pulp and dark, tart juice
our dyed eyes dart, bright birds
intent upon their brilliant foraging

thorns sketch on arms the face of theft
bees prick through branches webbed
and drooping, dusty, still as cloud

II

By evening, when recalled at last
each berry wore a gown of fine gray fur
we left them in the darkening grass

but what we took and threw away was not
what we desired, what we intended not weeping
baskets, bare branches, the aches we kept

but bending, rising, sweating, resting
we wanted day's green gathering together
the satisfaction of a mislaid need

YOUNG WOMAN CAUGHT READING IN AN EASY CHAIR

Thoughts on a photo, circa 1948

Perhaps the radio was playing, perhaps not.
It was at first difficult to say. Everything
happened too quickly, and we were struck
by other details—the room's modest disarray,
the portraits framed upon the yellowed,
spotless walls beside the crisply drawn drapes,
the ivy twining beyond its pot like a fashion
disaster, an unsuccessful hair-do tossed
in tangled dishevelment across the polished veneer
of the usually stolid, typically silent radio
and over its sides, as though shushing it—
like cartoon ivy with its finger in a socket,
so shocked it seemed by what it heard.
How the plush easy chair in which she sat
wore like old pajamas a pair of frayed,
unbecoming towels removed only when company
was coming. And how this young woman
seemed not to have been expecting any, her hand
clamped across her mouth in mock chagrin,
genuine surprise, and a pleasure that could not help
escaping from eyes just lifted from a magazine.

Certainly, such details should have told us something,
as should her scuffed gray saddle-shoes,
her anklets and dungarees, their cuffs
rolled up to mid-calf. As might the way she sat
sprawled across this chair, one leg
hooked inelegantly over an antimascaraed arm,
slouching as any parent would have told her not to—
especially when visitors might at any time arrive,
as we have, and the room moreover such a mess
("disaster area," one can almost hear
a scolding voice apologize), a litter of magazines
piled on her lap in a glamorous confusion
of fashion do's and don'ts, dating tips, and famous faces.

If we listen, perhaps we can hear what it is

that radio has been leaking into this cozy room.
Jazz, is it? The Hit Parade? Some soap?
One cannot quite say, any more than one knows
who may have entered this room with us,
catching this young woman so off-guard
to throw her into such delightful consternation.
It couldn't have been us she suddenly saw,
part of her mind still preoccupied perhaps
with Frank Sinatra, Rosemary Clooney,
in the new P.G. Wodehouse September *Cosmopolitan,*
for she was, beyond dismay, so clearly pleased,
and us she doesn't even know.
It was literally a question of who
she has eyes for, of who has been ushered in quietly
as an object lesson about always
behaving like a lady (to say nothing
of that get-up). No, it was not we
who had arrived hours or days early for a date
or something surely of this sort—
for she would not have been so disconcerted
had the visitor been a girlfriend,
nor so excessively gratified were the guest
merely a family acquaintance.

          One wanted,
regardless, to whisper (gesticulating laughably
from behind the new arrival, hands
a busy pantomime of cleaning), "Quick!
let's get this room picked up, turn off
that radio, hide those magazines, stuff
those towels beneath the cushion—and do
hurry up and change!" But it was already
too late for that, too late to do anything
about that hair, that "bird's nest." So at least,
"Sit up straight!" (in which remark
she could not have helped hearing,
"what would people think if they saw you
sitting here this way?")

          And for her
it is more than like being caught unawares

by a photographer and frozen in just the pose,
the clothes, in which she would want most
not to be remembered. Look—
even her calves are blushing (though this is
partly from pleasure, is a part of her pleasure),
one magazine sliding embarrassed
to the floor to join the mounting evidence
against her, its garish paper voice
in chorus with the dungarees and displaced doilies
taunting, "Yes, this is what she's really like!"

And everyone perhaps consents, although
possibly someone silently adds, "And better
than anyone could have imagined."
Except, perhaps, for Frankie, whose face
smiles up at us from the well-thumbed pages
of a magazine and who seems always to have known
all about such things as radios and movie stars
and young women left, then caught alone,
his approving voice having stepped softly
from the static-riddled speaker long minutes ago
to move easily as fancy about the room.

RIDDLE

child's grave, Easter

Stuffed animals in the damp, evangelical grass,
dying daffodils and lilies, an unassembled kite
speak of love's promise, which does not stop.

Unable to stay, the assembled depart
to stuff themselves with promised cold cuts,
kite checks to Christ, and dream of flight.

But all such dreams are checked, stall,
fall to earth. We nose forward, unable to stop
the cut from bleeding or get the dark to part.

This earthen child doubtless won't take root.
Even the reasonable flowers for all their cold
beauty wilt, glum with their own conundrums.

The pink and yellow animals grow sodden
as day sinks beneath its weight of disbelief.
Somewhere old gone Christ knows why.

Puzzled, one might pray, root for lovely
answers, find some pink aunt or jaundiced uncle
to rehearse what green Easter is about.

Elsewhere, damp eyes cry uncle, beautiful
speech blossoms. This child within its hearse
of dirt knows neither dark nor doubt.

DETROIT DROPS TWO TO CLEVELAND

The old man sits in his son's garage,
his life in boxes behind him,
Detroit's humiliation playing to the evening.

He drinks his coffee, listens, forgetting
the score, watching the street, children
lofting balls or cheering runners home.

The radio blares, but the Tigers are fading:
this game is over before it's over.
He can pick it up because his team is on the road.

A CARDINAL

From gutter,
fence post, branch,
a cardinal
worries the morning,

cries above
his fledgling, left
in tatters
by the terrier.

Were Cotton
Mather alive, he
could say
what this means.

ONE TUESDAY

I

Heartbreak that can be told
        is not the eternal heartbreak

the Tao must be wrong
        about needing
                to be free
                of desire
        to realize
        the mystery

bent beneath desire
        I ride enigma's very train

II

Hearts that break are doubtless
        hearts that break
                that doubt
        bottom out
                in mystery, desire
desire
        name themselves darkness

without darkness
        no light
                no chance to know one dwells
        in mystery whose home
                is heartbreak
        whose city is here

In pain indifferent to pleasure
        indifference to pain, my pleasure
                and my day
        seeded as the wind blows
        trained in loss

I am no sage
         rather refugee, castaway, child
         wren, sparrow, common mullein

I blossom less often
do not sing as I fly

III

How to use this heartache
         to stand firm
         to while away the hours

to let go of heartbreak
is to be wretched

I want only
         what Sappho
                  wanted
                  long ago
                  on the Aegean:
         to sleep upon my soft
                  girlfriend's breasts

IV

Not anthrax, plague
         the man who has my name
                  on some list
         rubble and flame
                  raised fist, flown flag
         blue of the departing train

heartbreaking
         the doll pulled from wreckage
         faces of baffled children, the call
                  never made, birds gone
                  forever elsewhere
         your face

but not the eternal heartbreak
            without name or place to be
                    set down
            holding the shape of flowers
            when there are no flowers

eternal heartbreak is not
            what fills this page
            is what these words do not conceal
            is what they cannot say

eternal heartbreak
            uncreates what is only made
lasts forever and helps
            by taking everything

V

The sparrow
            is a pretty bird
no city
            is an island

if I write another word
I will never understand

V

Heartbreak like water
finds the low places
easily spills
                    or hardens
                                        look
at how the lost
float, sport, drown
at how the happy recoil
from what is wet

on the Brazos
no more cane
no sun in the pines

only wind
four commandeered planes

then the sky
quiet   empty   blue
all of this and you
your breast
your face
and all the rest

POEM INTERRUPTED BY LACK OF LIGHT

for Jordan

I

Elsewhere rain blew in. There was nothing left to say, and no one would
shut up. Just a few miles away, newspapers were repeating their dirt. We
stood amid the gas station's well-lit squalor, eating ice cream. We would
have walked, but where we were, there was nowhere to go.

II

         Here, where
    the split wood burns
who would think
     that this might be
        the last good time

     with war
and you
    growing older
      but for now
         asleep beside me

     after how many pages
        by lantern light
    of your book
       and mine

     the Northern Cross
       overhead
     Lake Erie
       shushing
          beyond the trees

III

When the coffee boiled over
    it was done

       hot, strong, full of grounds

good drunk beneath a moon
       busy washing out
            night's bright clothes

your breathing steady   and deep
       an echo
           of the lake

your sleeping body
     warm, your face
        entirely beautiful

IV

the lantern
     dims, gutters
        campfire collapses
           orangely upon itself

despite moonlight
       Aldebaran
         shining
            Saturn rising

the night quiet
     only the lake
       and something
         in the underbrush

GIRL ON A HORSE

I

She sits astride a mild beast
as though posing for her future:

a horse, smear of grass, this girl
holding the reins like performing

some trick. She seems saddled
by disappointment, stalled, blown out

on the trail, her face a question
to which time is the answer.

The future, too, beneath a low sky
poses questions of its own:

what is it you want, cowgirl?
do you know the way home?

II

What does it mean to straddle
this horse, saddle and bridle?

Where is the barn and his straw-
strewn stall? Where is your bed?

Didn't anyone tell you, cowgirl,
the trail is awash, you're alone,

and more rain always threatens?
That no one ever returns all the way?

No need to protest, however,
about what love can do. All's well.

The trick is not difficult: if you
are going through hell, keep going.

PATRIOT ACT

Attached is a list of next
fall's cancelled freedoms.

Listen: they are the republic's
swan song, its dying fall.

Is it right that what is left
in our listing heads

has lost the will to course
through what we have lost

to the dustbin of history,
to the coarse *what gives?*

—victims of the give-and-take
of yesterday's tug-of-war . . .

Tug on the attached list, its dusty
wares, its wars, its whens and whys,

and it will pull away, our
birthright a mess of leftovers

now gone like some song,
like some lecture, say, on dust.

THE END OF MODERNISM

The sky hangs black in the pot's dark pool. I turn to offer you a cup, but you say you've had enough of stars.

Dawn: ice and sawed limbs strewn across the floor of morning, frozen ripples where angels disappear into the brine.

Why all this laughter amid so much debris? Your letters never explained, and helpless above the sink, I can only continue scrubbing these lines until they shine like some angel's wave-washed face, but chipped and crazed.

Down where the sky pours sympathetically into its cup someone is singing about the hangman's beautiful daughter, causing the chokecherry to sag, then break into pieces that sparkle like stars, like sea foam, like dishwater, that scatter like notes across this ancient kitchen floor.

FORCING BED

She wants the beans out early
to see them stretch, break earth, and climb—
grumbles at two planned rows of radishes
which neither of us likes
soon they'll clot the ground with white, hot roots
that will crack, spring seed, and rot

but I plant anything that does its growing underground—
potatoes, carrots, turnips, beets—
private, misshapen, dirty
taking time, not
dangling in the air from stake-held strings

*   *   *

She loves to see creation forming
persuasively in the humid air
swaying, green

I need to know it's happening
in the ground beneath me
fretfully, unseen

THE BULL, THE DOG, THE HORSE

*". . . at times he shows us what the bull felt, what the dog thought,
what the horse was imagining."*
 —Constantine Leontiev, commenting on Tolstoy

I: THE BULL

The bull pities Ivan Ilyich and the man
who did not know how much land a man needs,
but is perplexed by all those Russian names
as he is when cowboys sing about dogies
or when the steers make jokes about bulldozers.

Eyeing the steers, the bull feels superior, cocky,
pizzle-ready for any teat-heavy, cudsy cow,
yet doubtful when he contemplates Leviticus,
Bulfinch's Mythology, or his place in history;
vaguely ashamed when passing the china shop.

The bull loathes Kansas City, Chicago, Spain,
grows anxious when children climb the fence
and threaten to enter his grassy domain,
approves of bully pulpits and bully boys,
Picasso, Merrill Lynch, Noah and his ark.

II: THE DOG

The dog thinks *War and Peace* is bull,
prefers Charles Dickens and the slighter works
of Thomas Mann, thinks all thought
about what dogs might think is "bosh"
(such is the dog's way with a phrase).

When not absorbed with the Russians,
the dog thinks mostly about squirrels,
beef bones and strangers passing by,
his stuffed frog, closed doors, and how
the sunlight moves all day up the stairs.

In a brown study whose burden is fetching,
the dog suddenly entertains a new thought—treats!
How he dances for them at night, and how,
if on the sunless stairs he found us dead,
he'd bark until hoarse, then eat us raw.

III: THE HORSE

The horse doggedly imagines the most usual things—
pastures, steppes, Cossacks and cowboys,
Charlemagne, Custer, Crazy Horse, broughams
and Conestoga wagons, Silver and Trigger,
war upon war and furrow after furrow.

Glued to his imaginings, the horse improvises
the difference between "Turgenev" and "turgescent,"
imagines hack work giving one a charley horse,
fancies entertaining gluteal Anna Karenina,
the handsome Vronsky, along the Chisholm Trail.

Wondering what it must be like to be man's
best friend, to be cannonaded or gored, one horse
strays into a dream of a terrified small girl who,
clinging to his sunny mane, rides his ample back
bravely in slow circles all the way to joy.

IN OHIO

I

He walks across his fields
careful of meanings
impressed by thunder
silent in the rain

through tedious tractor afternoons
dreams of bumper harvests
and of drought
of corn-green rows well tended

picking up a clod of dirt
he worries it to soil
listening to the land
speak its leafy language

then cuts a melon tapped for days
before it answered, ready
waiting, eating, which was better
he couldn't say

II

Dusk, and crickets come alive
cornflowers glow
with fireflies aflirt above them
as fields grow dim

then fog, and nothing
save fog
and through it, crickets
crying for love

closing his eyes
he sees the still corn growing
half-asleep, thinks
I love this as the fish the pond

through the night, crickets
waking, he hears them
until the fog lifts
from morning's fields.

MEN PLAYING CATCH AT THE BEACH

They have brought their gloves along
with the children and wives, girl friends,
the cooler and blankets, as though
this is how a man tans.
                          They
are throwing the ball around,
calling a game in their heads,
pretending ease as they backpedal,
squint against the sun, sweat
as though still at work,
carefully indifferent to missed
chances, dropped cans of corn,
sending small apologies in the direction
of overthrows, behaving
as though expertise
were a possession not qualified
by performance.

                        They are so cocky,
proffering advice to the kids,
girl friends they permit to play,
rehearse in gasps between catches
their sporting lives, shouting
encouragement to each other,
good-natured epithets that sound
like passwords.

                        After twenty years
of school, jobs and families,
they still have or lack what it takes,
still, by God, know how
to pound a pocket, throw a ball.

SHECHINAH

for George W. Bush

Crazed man passes a café where
at six tables in the sun
of a late afternoon in May
in our nation's capital, six woman
sit drinking coffee

Windmilling his arms, he's after a
bit of God force, of brash
poetry, of sustaining passion—wants, as
he croons it, "to sex them
all night long"

They do not look up, they
do not stop turning the pages
of their books, do not stop
sipping, swallowing; indeed, they
now swallow harder

ARARAT FROM THE FLOOD

I

now the man in the ash-covered coat
turns again our way, still crowing fire

& now something hovers over the still ashes—
it comes for the dove, for the sparrow

it comes amid the green airburst of spring
while sparrows wheel above the feeder

and in Iraq the few, the proud, are vandalizing Ur,
birthplace of Abraham, poetry, the wheel

as it comes, earnest doves in the streets of our cities
block traffic for a few crumbs of peace

with their block-letter signs and their wonder,
their chants and their heartbreaking satyagraha

meanwhile, the branches, terrible with crows,
are breaking, chance bombs explode indifferently

indifferent, too, the buildings as they crumble,
the pictures aflame on the walls, the birds

II

now begins the sohbet between pulverized stone
and flesh, obscene terror and indecent empire

"lift the stone and you will find me" is what
the fliers of the missing say and say

"I have been away from my own soul,"
said Moulana Rumi, that rapt flyer, his words

still wrapped in the spring winds that arrive
masterfully one morning, vivant and scented

observe this scene: there are mournful symbols
and depleted morals everywhere we turn—

in the sparrows last seen in the lilac's bare branches,
the doves amid the shit and seed beneath the feeder

it is more than we can bear: Paula on CNN,
Black Hawks and Kalashnikovs, Saddam and Bush

today the bushes remain loud with birds:
what must happen to make us change our lives?

IRAQ WAR, DAY SIX

Didn't I see you
At the mall last Sunday?

SPRING NIGHT IN KENT, OHIO

For Ginny

We here in Kent say sleep when the oaks sleep
and the backyard is quick with dark,
when the fast-food restaurants close and the dogs
that flank us on the couch have lost their bark,
when beyond our rooftops wintry Orion leaps.

But when the moon, rising above our street,
illumines the bed, and your hip and flank become
a dune beyond the lightless huts of Hamdan,
I cannot sleep or be of Orion's love-glum,
restless mind despite our two dogs at my feet.

I am rather for your eyes, twin oases, green stars
seen from an open window on the moon.
I am hungry for the orchard of your thighs,
thirsty for the kashkul between, that boon
nourishing as welcome news and spring rains are.

How can I forgo in dreams the planetary night,
that sweeping orison between one day and the next
in which lilac and dogwood and iris open suddenly
and you await amid shadows like a sacred text
to be read by touch beneath a pale lunar light?

The moon gladdens the concealing oaks that rise above
all barking hunters and their dogs. In its glow
we are safe from the sin-sick world that sent us
upstairs sad, that lorn mirage beyond our window
behind which in Kent we lie fast awake in love.

STOPPED BY THE STARS

I

A few stars move across the night
like freight trains passing slowly
through the darkened fields above
past the nodding fields below
whose lights are folded flowers

II

Husbands and wives will rise with the dew
to dig in gardens, remove slips from coldbeds
string lines for peas and beans
will return to harvest cauliflower and, later, carrots
to cut zinnias for kitchen tables
and mums for bookcase vases

III

The iris purpling
the rise and fall of water
the dropping of an apple
to brittle grass

IV

Sunflowers stand with morning-glory vines entwined
pecked-at heads bent with the weight of weeks
yet looking still like beanstalks
that might be climbed to May
when peas were secure

V

No matter what happens
July earth falls warm through the gardener's fingers
birds get most of the sunflower seeds
and Orion still must wait until November
to confiscate the evening sky

VI

Like tended acts stars travel
and will arrive, perhaps, tomorrow

THE LEONIDS

17 November 2001

Our daughters drift beyond us.
They are growing up—sometimes
just another way of saying "apart"—
so are not with us tonight where
from a hot tub we don't mind

not sharing, far from them
we wait, watch beneath
a moonless sky so full of stars
it's difficult to locate Leo
behind the almost leafless oaks.

No matter: stars are falling
at a rate of 1200 per hour—
faint peripheral flarings, brief
pyrotechnic chars that cast quick
shadows, leave afterimage arcs.

Earth is wading what NASA
scientists call the "river of rubble"
Comet Tempel-Tuttle strews
across our path every 33 years.
Each November we enter it.

What happens then depends upon
"debris swarm" density, longitude,
and how the earth goes around the sun.
What happens has to do with how
what goes around comes around,

with how we long to be pulled in
by something and not drift,
with how we refuse loss, approve
the light, long for reunion,
for moments brighter than the moon.

After your blouse and jeans blazed
across my line of sight, and you
stepped into this tub beside me,
for two hours we weren't for a second
apart but centered, looking up,

working at 1200 kisses an hour,
300 for each daughter who is not
here to have her shadow cast,
secure knowing tomorrow the stars
will be right where we leave them—

the Big Dipper still pointing
the way to Polaris, the Sickle
of Leo, Orion with his dogs,
the Pleiades still two sisters more
than we have daughters.

Some nights we would stand
in this dark a long time
to see them again.
Unlike Tempel-Tuttle, their
reappearance is unpredictable.

They are here, then gone, then back.
We are left with the dust that,
not quite reaching us, showers
tonight with light—like some part
of ourselves we thought we'd lost.

Somewhere Comet 55P chases
its tail. We are at mutual perihelion,
and observing you by starlight
toweling off, I have a bright idea. Alone,
We seem to be thinking of nothing else.

L'ENVOI

I

Weeds in Winter—
a book by Lauren Brown
a field guide
for blasted fields
                    the pages
the way pages get
when they have gotten wet
then dried

a present once
inscribed with something
about forever
on page thirteen
                    this promise:
"the plants have
by no means
disappeared"

II

My knees are stiff
as I walk to the feeder
atop snow a brief thaw
and a hard freeze
have turned to ice
past last year's chicory
the defeated tick clover
that can be known
by its hairy pods
   its lima-bean shaped seeds

some spilled seed
          millet, cracked corn
dances away
across spilt sunlight
into what is left
of the poisonous Jimson

the wild sensitive
          whose leaves fold up when touched
          whose pods spiral upon opening
where house finch and winter wren
my coming scared away
          the inconspicuous brown creeper
          with its soft, lisping call
will find it

III

Nothing is ever wasted
although nothing lasts
I've a lump in my throat
no one likes the look of

I've things going wrong
I didn't know could go wrong
& will soon be identifiable
by the scar on my neck

ultrasound, up-take scan, biopsy
but today I walked on water
at fifty, I am as old as DNA
as young as anything with feathers

crush me, and like the tansy
beside the fence
you will still find
some scent

Notes

The dedication may be translated, "when I look at you, a beautiful poem always floats into my mind."

My epigraph is taken from William Gass's *Finding a Form.*

The final line of "The Lecture on Dust" is taken from Daniel Thompson's *Even the Broken Letters of the Heart Spell Earth.*

Like many others, I had my facts wrong regarding who did the deed when I wrote "For a Jogger Attacked in Central Park." See Patricia J. Williams, "Reasons for Doubt," *The Nation* 30 December 2002: 10.

The line in "Interview with a Suicide" about the moonlight going crazy is doubtless a memory-mangled appropriation of a line from Jonathan Edwards' song "Margaret." His line is better, so he shouldn't mind.

The nine poems comprising "Shoshaku Jushaku" were written under the influence of Shunryu Suzuki's *Zen Mind, Beginner's Mind*...and, of course, that of the woman they pursue. Stanza three of part five ends with lines lifted from three songs: Alejandro Escovedo's "Broken Bottle," Jimmie Rodgers' "Dreaming with Tears in My Eyes," and Bob Dylan's "Don't Think Twice." The first stanza of part six ends with and modifies a remark once made by Gary Snyder, who (if I recollect correctly) confessed to having himself borrowed the observation from a friend.

"Calling Time" was inspired by a photograph in Terry Pluto and Tony Kubek's *Sixty-One: The Team, the Record, the Men*; in the photograph—a public-ity shot—Rollie Sheldon and manager Ralph Houk pretend to listen to and admire the watch Rollie has been awarded as the most promising rookie at spring training.

Dorothy Fuldheim ("In a Neighborhood of Dying Light") was a Cleveland newswoman and media personality whose editorials appeared for several years as part of the local evening news on WEWS-TV.

The opening of "One Tuesday" improvises upon the opening lines of the *Tao Te Ching* as rendered by Stephen Mitchell. Other appropriations and allusions here are too obvious to note.

"Satyagraha" ("Ararat from the Flood") is Gandhi's term for "living in truth."
In the same poem "Moulana Rumi" is a reference to the Persian poet,
sometimes known as "our master Rumi." "Sohbet" is meant in the sense of
"mystical conversation" (definition courtesy of Coleman Barks).

"Plastic Fantastic Lovers" is the slightly altered title of a 1967 song by the
Jefferson Airplane.

The "shechinah" means "the feminine Divine" (Rebbe Mordechai Gafni).

"Spring Night In Kent, Ohio" was inspired by the Iraqi poet Saadi Youssef's
"Night in Hamdan" as translated by Khaled Mattawa. I should also like to
point out that although the "kashkul" is popularly known as a "beggar's
bowl," it was in fact a vessel used on special ceremonial occasions—and
that is the sense in which I am using it.

Brooke Horvath grew up in Elyria, Ohio, once home of playwright Robert E. Lee and of Sherwood Anderson, who wisely left town to become a writer. After graduating from Elyria High School, Horvath worked a variety of jobs—factory, road-crew, tasks less savory—while attending Kent State University, the State University of New York at Binghamton, and Purdue University, from which he received his Ph.D. in 1987.

The father of two daughters, Susan and Jordan, and step-daughters Emily and Caitlin, he makes his home in both Kent, Ohio, and Fredonia, New York, where his wife, Virginia, is Vice-President of Academic Affairs at the State University of New York, Fredonia.

Presently he is Professor of English at Kent State University, where he has taught since 1988. Horvath specializes in modern and contemporary American and world fiction and literary theory. Recent work includes *Understanding Nelson Algren* (University of South Carolina Press); *Line Drives: 100 Contemporary Baseball Poems* (Southern Illinois University Press), edited with Tim Wiles of the Baseball Hall of Fame; *"The Finer Thread, the Tighter Weave": Essays on the Short Fiction of Henry James* (Purdue University Press), co-edited with Joseph Dewey; and *Pynchon and Mason & Dixon* (University of Delaware Press), co-edited with Irving Malin.

Horvath's poems and essays about poetry have appeared in a variety of books and periodicals including *American Literature, American Poetry Review, Denver Quarterly, Journal of the American Medical Association, Poetry, The Prose Poem,* and *Sewanee Review.* His previous collections of poetry include *Consolation at Ground Zero* (Eastern Washington University Press) and the chapbook *In a Neighborhood of Dying Light,* which appeared as part of the chapbook anthology *Men and Women / Women and Men* (Bottom Dog Press).

Printed in the United States
69894LV00004B/58-75